BUILDING THE EARTH

BUILDING THE EARTH

PIERRE TEILHARD DE CHARDIN

DIMENSION BOOKS
WILKES-BARRE, PA.

Published by Dimension Books
Wilkes-Barre, Pa.

This is the first American edition of *Construire la Terre* by Pierre Teilhard de Chardin, originally published by Editions du Seuil (Paris). This edition was designed and illustrated by Sister Rose Ellen, C.S.C., St. Mary's College, Notre Dame, Indiana, who was assisted by Sr. Miriam Ann, C.S.C., Sr. M. Rosaleen, C.S.C. and Imry Szucs, of the staff of St. Mary's. The translation was made by Noël Lindsay, whose work was officially approved by the *Association of Friends of Teilhard de Chardin*.

Library of Congress Catalog Card Number 65-25559

The Age of Nations is past.

The task before us now,

if we would not perish,

is to build the earth.

P. Teilhard de Chardin

was born in France in 1881, in the Province of Auvergne. He entered the Society of Jesus in 1899 after finishing his secondary education at the Jesuit College of Mongré, near Lyons. In 1911 Teilhard de Chardin was ordained to the Catholic priesthood.

From the time of his ordination, this exceptional man dedicated himself to the study of the earth sciences, and above all to paleontology. Years of travel in China and elsewhere enabled him to advance his scientific aims, to make distinct contributions to the paleontological problem of the origins of man. Teilhard's daring scientific formulations were often couched in brilliant poetic language, as for instance his famous dictum that "man is the ascending arrow of the great biological synthesis."

In 1946, Teilhard de Chardin returned to Paris, and then in 1951 came to New York. Philosophers have remarked how congenial the thought of Père Teilhard is to the American temperament, given the predisposition Americans have to emphasizing the importance of matter in the fact of life. American educators, together with many church leaders of every faith, men of science as well as artists, literary people and those in political life rejoiced in his presence among us.

On Easter Sunday, April 10, 1955, Teilhard de Chardin died quite suddenly.

There appears from time to time among men an exciting genius, whose altogether personal, original and fascinating defiance of all categories is a challenge to men — creates a sea-change in the course of human thought. Such a man was Galileo or Descartes or Leibniz; and such a man was Pierre Teilhard de Chardin. In *Building the Earth,* which many believe to be the very heart of Teilhard's vision, there is expressed his political and moral and religious ideas about the future of man.

7

contents

FOREWORD

by Max H. Bégouën

of the *Association of Friends of Teilhard de Chardin*

A luminous scientific mind and a great heart, both of them big enough to encompass the whole world, gave Teilhard de Chardin the vision and the power, as long ago as 1937, to discern the rising tide of destructive forces which threaten our planet. And they led him to call on all mankind to unite in building the earth — in making the world a home for all peoples.

The peoples of the earth, "the natural units of humanity" as he called them, must (he declared) achieve earthly harmony through the very variety of their racial characteristics — characteristics which reciprocally enrich one another. He gave each of them this watchword: "Remain true to yourselves, but move ever upward toward greater consciousness and greater love! At the summit you will find yourselves united with all those who, from every direction, have made the same ascent. *For everything that rises must converge.*"

Just as the various cells and members of the body grow and unite to form a single living being and find their ultimate perfection only by constituting that being, so the constant goal of individual and national development should (in Teilhard's view) be the unity of mankind. Both individuals and nations must achieve this unity, he wrote, if we are ever to have any fulness of life on the earth.

This latter goal is still largely unattained, but there exists in all the countries of the world today a new ferment toward this end, a secret aspiration for what Teilhard perceived at a distance. May these countries be delivered from the fatal temptation of building for themselves alone; the sap which is rising in them is not destined to their own selfish ambitions but to the common achievement of all peoples, of mankind.

"The Age of Nations is past," wrote Teilhard. *"The task before us now, if we would not perish, is to build the earth."*

13

May there be an end to those hostile factions among us which stir up the forces of destruction to a frenzy. Let there be manifested instead a spirit of universal cooperation inspired by Teilhard's vision, by a passion to construct a world worthy of man. The value of any vision is not tested by force; it does not need the atom bomb in order to convince; its measure and its meaning are in the positive energies it can wrest from the womb of humanity. So Teilhard de Chardin taught us many years ago, and he affirmed further that above all the moribund ideologies there was one incomparably vast and powerful ideal. To this ideal he had devoted himself with all his heart, and his enthusiasm for it caused us to work with him for its fulfillment.

A social or ethnic group which can find no better answer to the tragic circumstances of life today than to increase its own selfish demands, shows by that very fact its own moral bankruptcy. By contrast love, which is the supreme form of human dedication and its greatest beauty, makes no demands; it simply strives and progresses. It realizes what the conditions of mankind should be and, brushing all obstacles aside, leads us onward to purify, elevate and fulfill the earth.

Despite the crushing burdens which selfish revolutions place on mankind today, the substance of a new world is being born in the very flesh of peoples all over the earth. Following in the steps of Teilhard, it is our task to bring this new world to fruition; to help the world concentrate all energies in the quest for peace; and in every country help prepare men who, at first in the circle around them and then at the head of nations, will preside over the true destiny of mankind.

We must in short be the vanguard of a crusade for human advancement, the call to which is sounded in the following pages by one who, from the summit he so heroically reached, caught a glimpse of the magnificence which might be the earth of man.

Max H. Bégouën

BUILOING THE EARTH

I we must save mankind

There is now incontrovertible evidence that mankind

has just entered upon the greatest

period of change the world has ever known.

The ills

from which we are suffering have had their seat

in the very foundations of human thought.

But today something

is happening

to the whole structure of human consciousness.

A fresh kind

of life is starting.

In the face of such an upheaval,

actually shaken by it,

no one can remain indifferent.

Swept along by the tide of affairs,

what can we do

to see clearly and

to act decisively?

No matter what reactions we may have to current events,

we ought first

to reaffirm a robust faith in the

destiny of man.

Even if that faith is already there,

it must be fortified.

It is too easy to find an excuse for inaction

by pleading the decadence of civilization,

or even the imminent end of the world.

This defeatism, whether it be innate or acquired or a mere

affectation, seems to me the besetting temptation of our time.

Defeatism is invariably unhealthy and impotent;

can we also prove that it is unjustified? I think so.

For anyone who can read the chart of facts

recorded by modern science,

it is now clear that mankind

is not an accidental phenomenon occurring by chance

on one of the smallest stars in the sky.

Mankind represents the culmination of the whole movement

of matter and life, so far as it is

within the range of our experience.

Is there any need to emphasize what strength

the believer derives from this recognition on the part of science

that the work

of creation is

a grand design of a Personal Being.

Man, the finished prototype

whose perfection makes everything prior to him

seem like a rough sketch

the keystone of the arch

toward which the architectonic lines

of the entire edifice converge,

Man, in these new perspectives

understands better

his title to the sovereignty of the universe.

Entirely different from the old anthropocentric view,

under which man was the static geometric center of the

universe,

this view that the "human phenomenon"

is the supremely characteristic form of the cosmic phenomenon

has an incalculable moral significance;

  it transforms our values, and

guarantees the permanency of the work which we are doing,

  or rather of the work which is being done through our agency.

  Today's critical events

mark a turning-point as well as a crisis

  in our understanding of progress.

  This we can and must believe; we are progressing.

  But in what direction are we moving?

  And, above all, what exactly is happening

  in the profound depths of human society?

We are progressing; let us suppose this to be true, but

  why is there still so much disorder around us?

  There are three major influences
  confronting each other

  and struggling for possession of the earth.

Democracy, Communism, Fascism [1].

Whence do these three forces derive their strength,

and why is the warfare between them so implacable?

In these three conflicting ideologies it is possible

to recognize clearly, though still not completely,

the three aspirations

which are characteristic of a faith in the future;

a passion for the future,

a passion for the universal

and a passion for the individual;

all three of them misunderstood,

. or imperfectly comprehended;

these are the three-fold main springs

which keep human energies in a state of tension

and conflict all around us

[1] The expression Fascism is used throughout to indicate all forms of authoritarian nationalism.

The case of Democracy is clear enough;

two faults of perspective, logically linked with each other,

have enfeebled and vitiated the democratic vision of the World,

one affecting its personalism,

and the other in consequence affecting its universality.

 The social aspirations of man cannot attain

full originality and full value,

except in a society which respects man's personal integrity.

Because this has not been understood

democracy rather than freeing man has merely emancipated him.

Hence the dispersion, strange as it may seem,

of a false liberalism both intellectual and social.

For with emancipation

each cell of society has thought itself free

to be its own center.

Hence, also, the disastrous equalitarianism which constitutes

a threat to any serious construction of a new earth.

Democracy, by giving

the people control over progress,

                    seems to satisfy the idea of totality.

In fact, it achieves only a counterfeit.

True universalism rightly claims to incorporate

all initiatives, all values without exclusion

all the most obscure potentialities of the person.

But it is essentially organic and hierarchic.

By confounding individualism and personalism,

crowd and totality,

by fragmenting and levelling the human mass,

democracy has run the risk of jeopardizing

our innate hopes for the future of mankind.

For that reason it has seen Communism break

away from it to the left,

and all the forms of Fascism rise

against it on the right.

In communism, faith in a universal vibrant humanity was,

at least in the beginning,

magnificently exalted.

The temptation of Russian neo-marxism

for the elite

consists far less in its humanitarian gospel

than in its vision of a totalitarian civilization

strongly linked with the cosmic powers of matter.

The true name of communism should be "terrenism".

Unfortunately, here too, the human ideal

was defective or very quickly became deformed.

On the one hand, in an excessive reaction

against the anarchic liberalism of democracy,

communism

soon arrived at the virtual suppression of the individual,

and has turned man into a termite.

On the other hand, in its unbalanced admiration

of the physical powers of the universe,

it has systematically excluded from its hopes

the possibility

of a spiritual metamorphosis of the universe.

The human phenomenon

(essentially defined by the development of thought)

was thenceforth reduced to the mechanical development

of a soulless collectivity.

Matter has veiled the spirit.

Pseudo-determinism has killed love.

The lack of personalism,

involving a limitation or even a perversion of the future

and undermining in consequence even the possibility

of universalism

such (rather than any of its economic reverses)

are the real dangers of Bolshevism.

There can be no doubt that the Fascist movement

was largely born out of reaction

to the so-called "ideas of the Revolution".

And this origin explains the compromising support

that it has not ceased to find among the numerous elements

interested

(for various social or intellectual reasons)

in not believing in a human future.

But passion is not inspired by stagnation,

and there is no lack of ardor in Fascism.

It is open to the future.

Its ambition is to embrace vast entities within its empire.

The sad thing

is that the sphere which it contemplates is restricted.

Fascism seems deliberately to overlook

 the vital human element,

 the unshakeable material basis,

 which, here and now, have already brought civilization

 into the international phase.

Fascism is obstinately determined

 to conceive and to build

 the modern world

 in the dimensions of a by-gone age.

 It gives preference to the race over mankind;

 it wishes to restore a soul to its own people,

 but it is indifferent to a soulless world.

It charts a course into the future

 in the search for forms of civilization

 which have vanished forever.

The forces which confront each other all around us

     are not purely destructive;

         each of them includes some positive constituents.

By virtue of these very constituents,

    they are unwittingly converging

      towards a common conception of the future.

      But in each of them the world

is struggling to achieve itself, striving to turn toward the light.

This is the crisis of birth, however, not the signs of death.

It indicates essential affinities, not eternal opposition.

      Once we have distinguished this much

    inside the currents and in the turmoil of history,

  we can determine the maneuver which will save us.

How can we unite all the positive values of civilization

    in a totality which will also respect individual values?

How can we attain that higher passionate unity

in which we shall find rooted and consummated

in a new synthesis

the Democratic sense of the rights of the person

the Communist vision of the potentialities contained in matter

and the Fascist ideal of an organized elite?

Fundamentally, in spite of the apparent enthusiasm

with which large sections of mankind go along

with the political and social currents of the day,

the mass of mankind remains dissatisfied.

It is impossible to find, either on the right or the left,

a truly progressive mind which does not confess

to at least a partial disillusionment with all existing movements.

A man joins one party or the other,

because if he wishes to act he must make a choice.

But, having taken his stand, everyone

feels to some extent hampered, thwarted, even revolted.

Everyone wants something larger, finer, better for mankind.

Scattered throughout the apparently hostile masses

which are fighting each other,

there are elements everywhere which are only waiting

for a shock in order to re-orientate themselves

and unite.

All that is needed is that the right ray of light

should fall upon these men as upon a cloud of particles,

that an appeal should be sounded

which responds to their internal needs,

and across all denominations,

across all the conventional barriers which still exist,

we shall see the living atoms of the universe

seek each other out,

find each other

and organize themselves.

In the old days our fathers set out on the great adventure

in the name of justice and the rights of man.

To us for whom new sciences have opened space and time

with dimensions unsuspected by our fathers

there are now new challenges.

We can no longer measure our efforts by old achievements,

no matter how exalting these were in their own time.

That is why our age is weary of the sectionalism which

confines human sympathies

in watertight compartments.

Such sectionalism drags us into an atmosphere

where it is no longer possible to breathe.

We must have air.

We must unite.

No more political fronts,

but one great crusade for human advancement.

The democrat, the communist and the fascist must jettison

the differences and limitations of their systems

and pursue to the full the positive aspirations

which inspire their enthusiasm,

and then, quite naturally, the new spirit

will burst the chauvinist bonds which still imprison it;

the three currents will find themselves merging

in the conception of a common task;

namely to promote the spiritual future of the world.

Only relative unanimity to start with;

but real unity,

to the extent to which all the world

is finally at one

in recognizing that the function of man

is to build and direct the whole of the earth.

Having lived for milleniums in self-contradiction,

Mankind has now reached a stage of development

from which it can,

with all its forces, advance forward.

It will be objected

    that in order to finally constitute

        a Crusade of Man,

    there must be some "antagonist" to oppose.

For my part, I do not believe in the

supreme effectiveness of the instinct of preservation and fear.

        It is not the fear of perishing,

        but the ambition to live

which has thrown man into the exploration of nature,

        the conquest of the atmosphere

        and the heavens.

The loadstone

which must magnetize and purify the energies in us,

whose growing surplus is presently dissipated

    in useless wars and perverse refinements,

I would place, in the last analysis,

in the gradual manifestation of some essential object,

whose total wealth,

more precious than gold,

more seductive than any beauty,

would be for man grown adult,

the Grail and the Eldorado

in which the ancient conquerors believed;

something tangible, for the possession of which

it would be infinitely good to lay down one's life.

For that reason, if a spiritual Human Front

began to come about,

it would need, alongside the engineers occupied in

organizing the resources of the earth

and its lines of communication

other "technicians" solely concerned

with defining and propagating the concrete goals, ever more lofty,

upon which the efforts of human activities

should be concentrated.

Until now, we have rightly been passionate

in seeking to unveil

the mysteries concealed in matter

infinitely great and infinitesimally small mysteries.

But an inquiry

of much greater importance to the future

will be the study of psychic currents and attractions;

a science of spiritual energy.

Perhaps, impelled by the necessity to build

the unity of the World,

we shall end by perceiving that the great object

unconsciously pursued by science

is nothing else than the discovery of God.

Humanity constantly risks

becoming absorbed in the secondary matter

of philosophic determinism and other mechanistic views of society.

But Christianity, speaking on behalf of man's conscience

maintains

the primacy of reflective thought

— it speaks for man as a free person.

This it does in the most effective of all ways,

not only by the speculative doctrinal defense

of the possibility of a centred,

but still universal consciousness,

but still more by transmitting and developing

through its mysticism

the meaning

and, in some sense, the direct intuition

of this center of total convergence.

The least that an unbeliever can admit to-day,

if he understands the biological situation of the world,

is that the figure of Christ

(not only as described in a book,

but as realized in the concrete

in the Christian consciousness)

is so far the most perfect approximation

to a final and total object

toward which the universal human effort can tend

without becoming wearied or deformed.

Note: *Father Teilhard de Chardin did not exclude from Christianity any one who expressly or implicitly believes in* Love. *He knew that the hour is not the same for every man to realize the essential love, cause and purpose of the universe.*

II   the spirit of earth

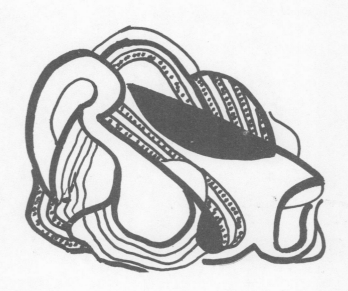

11 The Spirit of Earth

The phrase "Sense of Earth"

    should be understood to mean

        the passionate concern for our common destiny

          which draws the thinking part of life

                ever further onward.

In principle

    there is no feeling which has

          a firmer foundation in nature,

             or greater power.

But in fact there is also no feeling

    which awakens so belatedly,

  since it can become explicit only

when our consciousness has expanded beyond the broadening,

but still far too restricted, circles of family, country and race,

        and has finally discovered

  that the only truly natural and real human Unity

               is the Spirit of Earth.

Stimulated by consecutive discoveries

which in the space of a hundred years

have successively revealed to our generation several

important things

 — first the profundities and significance of time,

then the limitless spiritual resources of Matter,

and lastly the power of living beings acting in association —

it seems that our psyche is in the process of changing.

A conquering passion which will sweep away or transform

what has hitherto been the immaturity of the earth

has begun to show itself,

And its salutary action

comes just at the right moment

to control, awaken, or order

the emancipated forces of love,

the dormant forces of human unity,

and the hesitant forces of research.

a) Love.

Love is the most universal,

        formidable

    and mysterious of

        cosmic energies.

From the point of view of spiritual Evolution,

    it seems that we might be able

    to give a name and a value

    to this strange energy of love.

Could it not be, in essence,

    the attraction

    which is exercised upon each conscious element

    by the center of the universe?

The call toward the great union,

    whose attainment is the only real business

    in nature . . . ?

46

In this hypothesis

(which conforms with the findings of psychoanalysis)

love is seen

as a primitive and universal psychic energy

which gives significance to everything around us.

Thus, through woman

the universe

is really advancing toward man.

If man fails to recognize

the true nature

and the true object

of his love,

the disorder which follows

is profound and irremediable.

Stubbornly trying to gratify

    a passion which opens on the Infinite

   with something that is simply inadequate,

  man desperately tries to make up

for the fundamental disequilibrium brought about within him

  by a restless search for pleasures,

    especially those of a material character.

This is vanity

   and, in the eyes of anyone

who even partly perceives the inestimable value

   of the "spiritual quantum" of mankind,

    a frightening waste.

Look quite coldly,

as a biologist or an engineer,

at the reddening sky over a great city at night.

There, and indeed everywhere else,

the Earth is continuously dissipating in pure loss

its most miraculous power.

The earth is burning uselessly. Idly. Wastefully.

How much energy do you think

is lost to the Spirit of Earth in one night?

 Man must instead

perceive the universal reality

which shines spiritually through the flesh.

He will then discover

what has so far frustrated

and perverted his power to love.

Woman is put before him as the attraction

and the symbol of the world.

He can unite with her only by enlarging himself in turn

to the scale of the world.

And because the world is always larger,

and always unfinished

and always in advance of us,

to achieve his love

Man thus finds himself embarked

on a limitless conquest of the Universe.

In this sense, Man can reach woman only

through the consummation of the universal union.

Love is a sacred reserve of energy,

and the very blood stream of spiritual evolution;

that is the first discovery we can make

from the Sense of Earth.

b) Human Unity.

In singular opposition

to the irresistible attraction

manifested in Love

is the instinctive repulsion

which as a general rule

drives human beings like molecules,

away from each other.

This repulsion can in fact result

only from the timidity

or cowardice of an individual

in face of an effort of expansion

which would ensure his liberation.

What an increase

there is in his powers

when, in research

or in battle,

Man catches the breath of affection

or comradeship;

what fulfillment

when, in the instant of danger

or enthusiasm,

he finds in a flash that he has glimpsed

 the wonders of a kindred spirit.

These faint glimmerings

should help us realize

what a formidable power and joy

and capacity for action

still slumber in the human spirit.

Without any doubt men today suffer and vegetate in isolation;

they need a superior impulse to intervene

and force them to pass beyond the level

at which they are immobilized,

leading them to discover their profound affinities.

The Sense of Earth is the irresistible pressure

which will come at the right moment

to unite them in a common passion.

The love of interaction (far more important than even attraction)

governs different elements as they draw together

to sustain union.

Who can tell the plenitude of the yet almost unknown quality,

the immense fulfillment of fraternal friendships,

which, in the Noosphere, will accompany victory

over our internal divisions; that is to say

our recognition that human unity

can be advanced? can even be achieved?

c) Research.

The Spirit of Earth comes

> to explain to men

> > the reason

> > > for their superfluity of love,

> > > > and the way in which it might be put to use.

At the same time, it reveals itself as the force

> which is destined to set under way

> and organize the overwhelming mass

> > of human production and discovery.

> > Is the world condemned

> > > to perish in growing,

> > > > automatically stifled

> > > > > by the excess of its own weight?

By no means; but it is in the process

> of gathering the elements

> > > of a new and better body.

The whole question,

in this crisis of birth,

is the rapid emergence of the soul

which by its appearance will organize,

lighten and vitalize

this mass of stagnant and confused material.

But this soul can only be a "conspiracy"

of individuals who associate themselves

to raise to a new stage the edifice of life.

The resources we enjoy today,

the powers and secrets of science we have discovered,

cannot be absorbed by the narrow system

of individual and national divisions

which have so far served the leaders of the world.

The age of nations is past.

The task before us now, if we would not perish,

is to shake off our ancient prejudices, and to build the earth.

The more I look at the world as a scientist

    the less I see any other possible biological result

    apart from its active and conscious unity.

Life can progress on our planet in the future

    (and nothing will prevent it from progressing,

    not even its own internal servitudes)

    by throwing down the barriers

        which still wall off human activity,

    and by giving itself up without hesitation

        to faith in the future.

We must put in the forefront of our concrete preoccupations

    the systematic arrangement

    and exploration of our universe,

        understood as the true country of mankind.

Then material energy will circulate,

    and (more important still) spiritual energy,

    now corrupted by the petty jealousies of modern society,

    will find its natural outlet

in the attack launched against the mysteries of the world.

The time has come to realize

that research is the highest human function,

embracing the spirit of war

and bright with the splendor of religion.

To keep up a constant pressure

on the surface of the real,

is not that the supreme gesture of faith in Being,

and therefore the highest form of adoration?

All that is ours,

if we understand how to avoid

stifling within us the Spirit of Earth.

Whoever wishes to be part of this spirit

must die and be born again,

for others and for himself.

In order to reach this higher plane of humanity

he must bring about a complete transformation

in his whole sense of values and his whole action.

Yet a little while and the Spirit of Earth

    will emerge with its specific individuality

        and its own character and physiognomy.

And then, on the surface of the Noosphere,

    gradually sublimated in thought and passion,

        ever striving to solve more lofty problems,

        to possess greater objects,

        our tension towards being will be at its maximum.

What will happen at this critical stage

    in the maturation of terrestrial Life?

Are we going to be able at that moment

    to unite with other centers of cosmic life,

    to continue the labor of universal synthesis

        on a higher scale?

More probably, something else will happen,

    something which can be glimpsed only

when the influence of God is brought into the reckoning.

It would be nursing a great illusion

if the man of our times were to think

that, having attained a fuller understanding

of himself

and of the world,

he had no further need of religion.

There has been a multiplication of systems

in which the existence of religion

has been interpreted as a psychological phenomenon

associated with the childhood of mankind.

At its maximum

when civilization is beginning,

it should gradually fade away,

giving place to more positive constructions,

from which God

(particularly a personal and trancendent God)

would be excluded.

In reality,

    for those who can see,

the great conflict from which we will have escaped

    will only consolidate in the world

        the necessity of faith.

Having reached a higher degree of self-mastery,

    the Spirit of Earth will experience

        an increasingly vital need to adore;

out of universal evolution God emerges in our consciousness

    as greater and more necessary than ever.

The only possible Motive Power of a life

    which has reached the stage of Reflection

    is an Absolute, or in other words a Divine, Term.

Religion has sometimes been understood

    as a mere antidote to our evils, an "opiate"

Its true purpose is to sustain and spur on the progress of life.

It is the profound need of an Absolute,

sought from the start

 through every progressive form of religion.

Once this starting point is realized,

it becomes evident that the "religious function"

born of hominization and linked thereto

is bound to grow continuously with man himself.

The more man is man, the more he will feel the need

to devote himself to something which is greater than he is.

Is it not that which we can ascertain around us?

At what moment in the Noosphere

has there been a more urgent need

to find a faith, a hope

to give meaning and soul

to the immense organism we are building?

By the capital event of hominization

the most "advanced" part of the cosmos

found itself personalized.

This simple change in a variable

introduced for the future

a two-fold condition of existence

which cannot be escaped.

Since everything in the universe,

starting from Man,

takes place in the personalized being,

the ultimate Term of the universal Convergence

must also possess

(in a supreme degree) the quality of a Person.

To super-animate, without destroying,

a universe made up of personal elements,

he must himself be

a special Center.

Thus there reappears,

not as a matter of emotion or instinct,

but closely linked

with contemporary ideas on evolution,

the traditional conception of a God

exerting an intellectual influence upon immortal beings,

distinct from himself.

The current which raises matter

should be conceived less

as a simple internal impulse than as a tide.

The multiple rises,

attracted and incorporated

by the "Already One".

In the first phase—before man—

the attraction was vitally,

but blindly,

felt by the world.

Since man, it is awakened

(at least partially)

in reflective liberty

which sustains religion.

Religion

is not an option

or a strictly individual intuition,

but represents the long unfolding,

the collective experience

of all mankind,

of the existence of God—

God reflecting himself personally

on the organized sum

of thinking beings,

to guarantee a sure result of creation,

and to lay down exact laws

for man's hesitant activities.

III human ENERGY

H uman Energy presents itself to our view

as the term of a vast process

in which the whole mass of the universe

is involved.

In us

the evolution of the world towards the spirit

becomes conscious.

From that moment,

our perfection, our interest,

our salvation as elements of creation

can only be to press on with this evolution

with all our strength.

We cannot yet understand

exactly where it will lead us,

but it would be absurd for us to doubt

that it will lead us towards some end

of supreme value.

From this there finally emerges

in our twentieth century human consciousness,

for the first time

since the awakening of life on earth,

 the fundamental problem of Action.

No longer, as in the past,

for our small selves,

for our small family,

our small country;

but for the salvation and the success

of the universe,

how must we, modern men,

organize around us

for the best

the maintenance,

distribution

and progress

of human energy?

The first object

which should attract the attention

of the technician of human energy

is to ensure

to the human nuclei

taken in isolation,

their maximum of consistency

and efficiency as elements.

To perfect individuals so as to

confer upon the whole the maximum of power,

 that is the obvious line to follow

for the final success of the operation.

The organization of the human energy

of the element,

whatever its general methods may be,

must culminate

in forming at the heart of each element,

the greatest possible amount of personality.

But today,

while the mass formation of human society

is taking place under our eyes

and in our consciousness,

Man, assuming him to be henceforward fixed

in his individual nature,

can see a new and boundless field of evolution

opened up before him;

the field of collective creations,

associations,

representations

and emotions.

How can we lay down any limits

to the effects of expansion,

penetration and spiritual fusion

which would flow from the coherent ordering

of our human multitude?

This will be a capital phase of history,

    when all the transformed power

        of fleets and armies

  will come in to reinforce that other power

  which the machine age has lulled somewhat into idleness,

  and an irresistible tide of liberated energies

  will mount towards the most progressive circles

      of the Noosphere.

A substantial part of this tide of available energy

    will immediately be absorbed

   in the expansion of man in matter.

      But another part,

        and that the most precious,

      will inevitably flow back

    to the levels of spiritualized energy.

Spiritualized Energy is the flower of Cosmic Energy.

To dominate and canalize

        the powers of the air and the sea

                is all very well.

      But what is this triumph,

    compared with the world-wide mastery

    of human thought and love?

In truth, no more magnificent opportunity than this

      has ever been presented

        to the hopes and efforts of the earth.

        We are very ready

        to boast of living in a century

          of enlightenment and science.

        And yet the truth is quite the reverse;

    we are still lingering

    among rudimentary and infantile forms

        of intellectual conquest.

What proportion of activity in the world today,

in money, manpower and effort,

is devoted to exploring and conquering

the still unknown areas of the world?

At present most men still merely understand strength,

the key and symbol of violence

in its most primitive and savage form of war.

But let the time come, as come it will,

when the masses will realize

that the true human successes

are those which triumph

over the mysteries of matter and of life.

At that moment

a decisive hour will sound for mankind,

when the spirit of discovery absorbs all the momentum

contained in the spirit of war.

It represents in consequence

that part of human strength

which there is the greatest interest in organizing.

What are the main directions

in which we can imagine it tending?

And in which we can help it to develop,

starting in the heart of our individual natures?

No doubt in the direction of a decisive flourishing

of some of our old powers,

 accompanied by the acquisition

of some additional faculties,

and some extended consciousness.

Love, as well as thought,

is always in full growth in the Noosphere.

The excess of its expanding energy

over the daily diminishing needs of human propagation

is daily becoming more evident.

This means that love is tending,

    in its fully hominized form,

    to fulfill a much larger function

        than the mere call to reproduction.

Between Man and Woman,

    a specific and reciprocal power of sensitization

    and spiritual fertilization

        seems in truth to be still slumbering,

        demanding to be released

    in an irresistible upsurge

toward everything which is truth and beauty.

Beyond a certain degree of sublimation,

    by the unlimited possibilities of intuition

    and inter-relation which it brings,

        spiritualized love penetrates into the unknown.

In every field we will begin to live constantly in the presence

    and with the thought of the whole.

There is nothing more significant,

from the point of view of human energy,

than the spontaneous appearance,

and, ultimately, the systematic cultivation

of a "cosmic sense" of this kind.

Through such a sense,

Men cease to be self-contained individuals,

and join in a common cause.

In them, thenceforth, the spiritual energy of the element

is finally ready to integrate itself

in the total energy of the Noosphere.

But we must not fail to bring out an important point;

the perfection and usefulness

of each nucleus of human energy

in relation to the whole

depend in the last resort

upon whatever is unique and incommunicable

in each of them.

The great point

to which the technician of the Spirit

 should direct his attention

in dealing with human beings

is to leave them

the possibility of discovering themselves,

in the transformation

which he is seeking to bring about in them,

and the freedom to differentiate themselves

ever more and more.

The first lineaments of a common consciousness

contain in themselves a vital need

to make themselves clear

and to prolong themselves internally.

Intellectually, the progress of science

is proceeding to construct

a synthesis of the laws of Matter and Life,

which, fundamentally,

is nothing else but a collective act of perception;

the world seen in the same coherent perspective

by the whole of mankind.

Socially,

the fusion and intermingling of races

are leading directly to the establishment

of an equally common form,

not merely of language,

but of morality and ideals.

The organization of human energy,

taken in its entirety,

directs itself

and impels us

towards the ultimate formation,

above each personal element,

of a common human soul.

The conjunction of activities

out of which there will come a collective human soul,

supposes as its principle,

a common aspiration,

actuated by a common hope.

To set in motion

and sustain such human energy,

there must be at the origin

an attraction exercised

by a desired object.

Since there is neither fusion

nor dissolution

of individual persons,

the Center which they aspire to rejoin,

must necessarily be distinct from them,

that is, it must have its own personality,

its autonomous reality.

For its maintenance and operation

the Noosphere physically requires

the existence in the universe

of a real pole of psychic convergence;

a Center different from all other centers,

which it "super-centers" by assimilating them;

a Person

distinct from all other persons,

whom it fulfils

by uniting them

to itself.

The world would not function,

if there were not,

somewhere

outside time and space,

a cosmic point

of total synthesis.

We have just recognized it:

by hominization the universe

has reached a higher level,

where its physico-moral powers

gradually assume the form

of a fundamental affinity

which links individuals to each other

and to their transcendent Center.

In us and around us the elements of the world

go on unceasingly personalizing themselves

more and more,

by acceding to a Term of unification;

itself personal,

so much so,

that from this Term of ultimate confluence

there radiates and

to this term in the last resort

there flows back all the essential Energy of the World—

that energy which,

having generally agitated the cosmic mass,

emerges from it to form the Noosphere.

What name must be given to such an influence?

One only—Love;

Love, the supreme form

and the totalizing principle

of human energy.

Picture a man

who has become conscious

of his personal relations

with a supreme Person

with whom he is led to merge

by the whole interplay of cosmic activity.

In such a man,

and starting from him,

a process of unification is launched,

marked by the following stages:

— the totalization of every operation

in relation to the individual;

— the totalization of the individual

in relation to himself;

— and lastly, the totalization of the individual

in the collective Man.

All these so-called "Impossibilities" come about

under the influence of Love.

Omega,

He towards whom all converges,

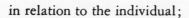

is concurrently

He from whom all radiates.

Impossible to place him as a focus

at the summit of the universe,

without at the same time diffusing his presence

in the intimate heart of the smallest movement of evolution.

What does that mean

except that,

for anyone who has seen it,

everything, however humble,

provided it is placed in the line of progress,

warms, enlightens and animates itself,

and in consequence

becomes the subject of total adhesion.

The fact that

under the animating influence of Omega

every one of our individual actions

may become total

 is in itself a marvellous use

of human energy.

But it transpires that, the first transfiguration of our activities

just barely launched, they tend to prolong themselves

in another even more profound metamorphosis.

By the very fact

that they become total,

each one individually,

our actions logically find themselves

induced to totalize themselves,

taken altogether in a single act.

Here is a veritable synthesis

which the love of Omega

brings about

on the combined cluster of our faculties:

In the superficial course of our existences,

there is a difference between

seeing and thinking,

understanding and loving,

giving and receiving,

growing and shrinking,

living and dying.

But what will happen to all these oppositions

when

their diversity is revealed in Omega

as the infinitely varied operation

of the same universal contact?

Without disappearing in the world

to the least degree

they will tend to combine

in a common resultant,

where their plurality,

still recognizable,

will flourish in ineffable richness.

Why should this astonish us?

Are we not familiar

in a less intense degree

with a perfectly parallel phenomenon

in our own experience?

When a man loves a woman nobly,

    the result of this overmastering passion,

        which exalts the being above itself,

    is that the life of that man,

        his power to create and to feel,

        his whole universe,

    become specifically contained

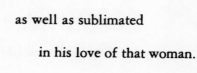

                as well as sublimated

                    in his love of that woman.

        And yet,

        woman,

however necessary to man,

        in order to reflect,

        reveal,

        communicate

    and "personalize" the world to him,

        is still not the center of the world!

If, therefore,

the love of one being for another

shows itself

powerful enough to fuse

(without confusing)

into a single impression

the multitude of our perceptions

and our emotions,

what vibration would not be drawn

by our beings from their

encounter

with Omega?

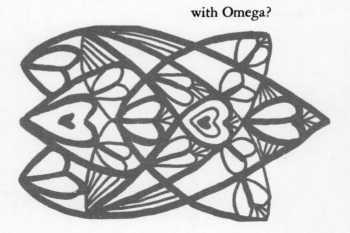

When,

    by the progress in our hearts

      of this love of the whole,

we come to feel,

      extending above the diversity of our efforts

        and our desires,

    the exuberant simplicity of an urge

      in which are mixed and exalted,

        without loss,

    the innumerable gradations of passion and action,

then in the heart of the mass formed by human energy,

    we shall each be approaching the plenitude

    of our effectiveness and our personality.

      To totalize without de-personalizing;

      to save at the same time

        the whole and the parts.

    Everyone agrees on this two-fold aim.

But how do existing social groups

grade the values

which in theory they are agreed

they want to preserve?

By regarding the person

as secondary and transitory,

and in placing at the head of their program

the primacy of pure totality.

In all the systems of human organization

which confront each other before our eyes,

the underlying assumption

is that the final state

towards which the Noosphere is tending

is a body without an individualized soul,

an organism without a face,

a diffused humanity,

an impersonal.

But this starting-point,

once admitted,

vitiates the whole subsequent course

of the operation

to the extent of making it impracticable.

How, if the universe finally tends

to become a thing

can it still find place for a Person?

If the summit of human evolution

is regarded as impersonal in character,

the elements which reach it

will inevitably,

in spite of all efforts

to the contrary,

see their personality shrinking

under its influence.

And that is exactly what is happening.

92

Those who work for material progress

or racial causes alone

strive in vain

to achieve freedom;

they are fated to be swamped

by the determinisms

they are constructing.

Their very method of thought mechanizes them.

And from that moment

there is nothing left

to control the operations

of human energy

but brute force

— the force which,

quite logically, some people to-day

would again like

to make us worship.

It is not brute force we need,

but love,

and therefore, as a start, the recognition

of a Transcendent

which makes universal love possible.

What will happen

on the day when,'

in place of the impersonal Humanity

put forward by modern social doctrines

as the goal of human effort,

we recognize the presence

of a conscious Center of total convergence?

At that time, the individuals

caught up in the irresistible current

of human totalization

will feel themselves strengthened by the very movement

which is bringing them closer together.

The more they are grouped

under a Personal,

the more personal

they will themselves become.

And that effortlessly,

by virtue

of the properties of love.

Picture an earth

where all men are clearly and primarily decided on

advancing together

 to a passionately desired Being,

in whom each recognizes

in what was most incommunicable in his neighbor

a living participation.

In such a world

    coercion would become unnecessary

    for the purpose of retaining individuals

      in the most favorable order for action,

  of orienting them in the full play of free will

      towards the best combinations,

making them

    accept the restrictions and sacrifices

    imposed by a certain human selection

and determining them in the end

    not to squander

      their capacity for love,

but to sublimate it jealously

    for the purpose of ultimate union.

We have reached a cross-roads in human evolution

  where the only road which leads forward

    is towards a common passion.

To continue

to place our hopes in a social order

achieved by external violence

would simply amount

to our giving up all hope

of carrying the Spirit of Earth

to its limits.

But human energy,

like the universe itself,

the expression

of an irresistible

and infallible movement,

could not be prevented

by any obstacle

from attaining freely

the natural term

of its evolution.

Therefore,

in spite of all the apparent improbabilities,

we are inevitably approaching

a new age in which the world

will cast off its chains,

to give itself up at last

to the power

of its internal affinities.

We must believe

without reservation

in the possibility

and the necessary consequences

of universal love.

The theory and practice of total love

have never ceased, since Christ,

to become more precise,

to transmit and propagate themselves;

so that with two thousand years

of mystic experience behind us,

the contact which we can make

with the personal focus of the universe

has gained just as much explicit richness

as the contact we can make,

after two thousand years of science,

with the natural spheres of the world.

Regarded as a "phylum" of love,

Christianity is so living

that, at this very moment,

we can see it undergoing an

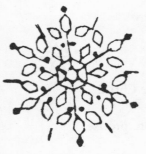

extraordinary mutation

by elevating itself

to a firmer consciousness

of its universal value.

Is there not

now under way

one further metamorphosis,

the ultimate one,

the passage of the circles

to their common Center,

the realization of God

at the heart of the Noosphere,

the apparition

of the "Theosphere"?

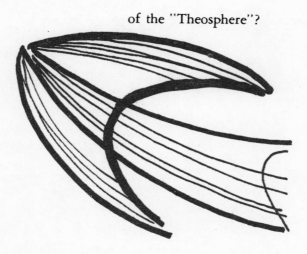

IV   thoughts on PROGRESS

It has become fashionable to-day

to mock or to treat with suspicion,

anything which looks like faith in the future.

If we are not careful

this scepticism will be fatal,

for its direct result

is to destroy

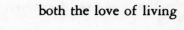

both the love of living

and the momentum of mankind.

Firmly based on the general history of the world,

as revealed to us by palaeontology,

over a period of 300 million years

we can make these two assertions,

without losing our foothold in dreams:

a) First and foremost,

    mankind still shows signs of a reserve,

        a formidable potential of concentration,

            that is, of progress.

Think of the immensity

    of the powers,

        ideas

        and persons

    not yet discovered

    or harnessed

    or born

    or synthesized.

    In terms

  of "energy"

and biology,

the human race is still very young and very fresh.

b) The earth is still far

from having completed

its sidereal evolution.

 True,

we can imagine

all sorts of catastrophes

which might intervene

to cut short

this great development.

But for 300 million years now,

Life has been going on paradoxically

in the midst of improbability.

Does that not indicate

that it is marching forward,

sustained by some complicity

in the motive forces of the Universe?

The real difficulty

which faces man

is not the certainty

that he is the seat of constant progress;

it is rather the conception

of how this progress

can go on

for a long time yet at its present rate,

without life exploding of itself

or blowing up the earth

on which it was born.

Our modern world

was created

in less than ten thousand years,

and in the last two hundred years

it has changed faster

than in all the previous milleniums.

The March Forward.

Progress,

    if it is to continue,

        will not happen by itself.

Evolution,

    by the very mechanism

      of its syntheses,

      is constantly

        acquiring greater freedom.

In practice,

    what steps must we take

        in relation to this forward march?

I see two,

    which can be summarized in five words:

        a great hope,

        in common.

108

a) First, a great hope.

This must be born spontaneously

in every generous soul

in face of the anticipated work,

and it also represents

the essential impetus

without which nothing

will be done.

A passionate love of growth,

of being,

that is what we need.

Down with the cowards and the sceptics,

the pessimists and the unhappy,

the weary and the stagnant.

b) In common.

On this point also

    the history of Life

        is decisive.

There is only one way

    which leads upwards;

        the one which,

            through greater organization,

            leads to greater

            synthesis and unity.

Here again, then,

    down with the pure individualists,

        the egoists, who expect to grow by excluding

            or diminishing their brothers

            — individually, nationally

              or racially.

Life is moving towards unification.

Our hope

will only be operative

if it is expressed

in greater cohesion

and human solidarity.

The future of the earth is in our hands.

How shall we decide?

A common science merely brings

the geometric point of

different intelligences

nearer together.

A common interest,

however passionate,

merely brings beings into indirect touch,

through an impersonal which destroys personality.

It is not our heads

or our bodies

which we must bring

together,

but our hearts.

The generating principle

of our unification

is not finally to be found

in the single contemplation

of the same truth

or in the single desire

awakened by something,

but in the single attraction

exercised

by the same

Someone.

v on the possible basis of a common credo

Once the reality of a Noogenesis

is admitted

(the concentration

and collective march forward

of human thought)

the believer in the world

finds himself obliged

to give a growing place

in his thoughts

on the future

to the values

of personality

and transcendence.

Of personality,

since a universe on the road of psychic concentration

is identically a universe which is becoming personalized.

And of transcendence,

because a last pole of "cosmic" personalization,

if it is to be supremely consistent

and unifying,

can hardly be conceived

except as emerging from elements

 which it super-personalizes·

by uniting them.

 Still in the same perspective,

assuming it is admitted

that there is a cosmic genesis

of the spirit,

the believer in heaven realizes that the mystic transformation

of which he dreams presupposes and confirms

all the tangible realities and laborious conditions

of human progress.

To be super spiritualized in God,

    must not mankind first be born

        and grow in conformity

        with the whole system

        of what we call evolution?

The sense of earth

    opening and flowering upwards

    in the sense of God,

        and the sense of God

    rooted and nourished from below

        in the sense of earth.

    The transcendent personal God

and the universe in evolution,

no longer forming two antagonistic poles of attraction,

    but entering into a hierarchic conjunction

        to uplift the human mass

            in a single tide.

Such is the notable transformation

which the idea

of the spiritual evolution

of the universe

implies in theory

and which is beginning

to come about in practice

in a growing number of minds,

free-thinkers as well as believers.

The very transformation we are seeking.

The new spirit for a new world.

To unify the vital human forces,

     so lamentably disunited at this moment,

        the direct and effective way

          would simply be

       to sound the alarm

        and to form a block

      of all those who

           either on the right

   or the left,

       believe that the great affair

       for modern mankind

         is to break its way out

         by forcing

     some threshold

         of greater consciousness.

Whether Christians or not,

   the men

      who are animated

         by this conviction

           form a homogeneous category.

      Although

        in the march of mankind

      they take their stations

    on opposing wings,

they can advance

        hand in hand,

      because their attitudes,

    far from being exclusive,

      virtually prolong each other,

      and ask only

        to be completed.

What

 are they waiting for,

  in order to set up

   the common front

    of all those who believe

    that the universe

     is moving forward,

 and that it is our task

  to make it

   move forward?

Would not this

   be the solid nucleus

  around which

    to-morrow's unanimity

     must

      develop?

In spite of

                      the wave of scepticism

                      which seems

              to have swept away

                      the hopes

              (over-simplified

        and over-materialist)

upon which the nineteenth century lived,

        faith in the future

              is not dead

                      in our hearts.

                              Better still,

                      it is this hope,

              deepened

        and purified,

              which seems bound

                              to save us.

It is not only

that the idea

of our consciousness

of a possible awakening

to a super-consciousness

daily

becomes better based

scientifically

on experience

and more necessary

psychologically

to keep alive

in man

the zest for action;

in addition,

    this very idea

        pushed

   to its logical conclusion.

      seems the only one

       capable

  of making mankind ready

  for the great event

      which we are awaiting;

     the discovery

    of a synthetic act

     of adoration

        in which are allied

         and mutually exalted

the passionate desire

to conquer

the world,

and the passionate desire

to unite ourselves

with God;

the vital act,

specifically new,

corresponding to a new age

of the earth.

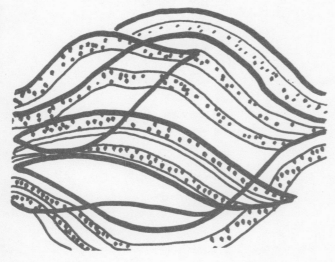